13 Art Inventions
Children Should Know

Florian Heine

PRESTEL

Munich · London · New York

Contents

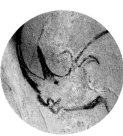

nventions change the world. Throughout history, clever people have come across ideas for how you can make something better or create something completely new.

Inventions are important in art too. Sometimes they are completely new ideas, such as an original way of painting something; and sometimes they are ideas that have nothing to do with art, but which have an important effect on art.

In this book you will find 13 inventions that changed art or helped to develop it further. Timelines will show you other things that were discovered or invented in art history. Some words that you may not know yet are explained in the glossary. And there are also tips, ideas, and suggestions for how you can find out more about all the inventions you see here. You will even find a few quiz questions to answer.

Have fun!

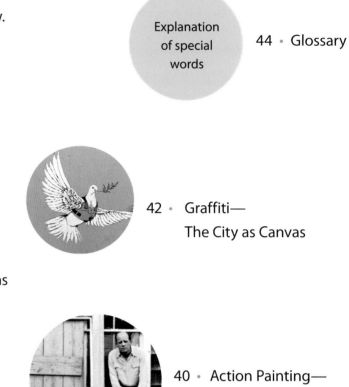

Explanation of special words

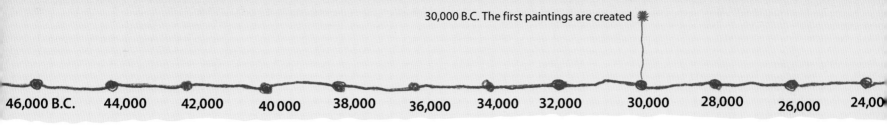

invention:
　Painting
invented by:
　Prehistoric People
Invented:
　About 15,000–30,000
　years ago
Place:
　Southern France

Painting—
Rhinoceroses in Europe

Pictures that are 15,000–30,000 years old have been found on the walls of caves in France and Spain. They mark the beginning of painting.

If we are talking about inventions in art, we should start at the very beginning of art itself. That was a very long time ago. To get an idea of just how long ago, try to imagine your great-grandfather; and then imagine another thousand "greats" on top of that. Then you would arrive back at the time when painting was invented, about 30,000 years ago.

In those days, the animals living in Europe were very different from the ones we know today: woolly rhinoceroses, mammoths, cave bears, giant deer called megaloceroses, and even hyenas. The people still lived in caves. And it was here that they began to paint the animals on the walls.

The first artists created their animal drawings with pieces of charred wood. To make them look more realistic, they added colors using different kinds of soils, ground stones, and plants. That was how they invented paints. They probably frayed the ends of branches to make paintbrushes.

All that is very impressive, but the paintings themselves are even more remarkable. As far as we know they are the oldest pictures humankind has ever produced. And you might think that because people had

4

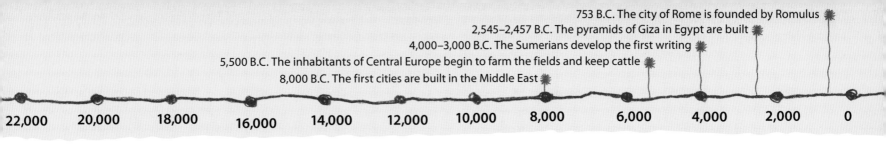

753 B.C. The city of Rome is founded by Romulus
2,545–2,457 B.C. The pyramids of Giza in Egypt are built
4,000–3,000 B.C. The Sumerians develop the first writing
5,500 B.C. The inhabitants of Central Europe begin to farm the fields and keep cattle
8,000 B.C. The first cities are built in the Middle East

| 22,000 | 20,000 | 18,000 | 16,000 | 14,000 | 12,000 | 10,000 | 8,000 | 6,000 | 4,000 | 2,000 | 0 |

Wall paintings in the cave at Lascaux
c. 15,000 B.C., Cave at Lascaux, Montignac

In a recreation of the cave at Lascaux, in southern France, you can experience for yourself what it must have felt like to live in a cave.

only just invented painting, they would perhaps not be very good at it yet. But you would be wrong! The first painters were real artists! They managed to paint animals on the cave walls that were so realistic, you might almost think they were alive.

Nowadays we do not know why those people so long ago painted pictures of animals on cave walls. They certainly didn't do it to make the walls look prettier, as we might do today by hanging up a poster or a picture in our room. The ancient paintings are found deep in the cave, where it is completely dark, and the people who made them would have possessed only a few torches to provide dim light. Such artworks were probably painted as part of a cult: the people in those days probably thought that the pictures possessed magic powers. They might even have believed that by painting certain animals, they could gain power over those creatures and hunt them more successfully. In fact, many ancient cultures saw magic in images, and things have not really changed to this day. Just think of all the photos of people we love. In reality, they are no more than lifeless images on paper. But we still look at these pictures when we feel lonely; and when we think of the people they represent, we may even feel a bit better. So pictures are more closely linked to our thoughts and feelings than we realize.

Rhinoceros
c. 30,000 B.C.,
Cave at Chauvet, near
Vallon-Pont-d'Arc

As you can see on this wall painting, there were rhinoceroses living in Europe 30,000 years ago, and some of them even had enormous horns.

The animal pictures that you can see on these pages were discovered in 1994 in the caves at Chauvet, France. They are about 30,000 years old and are very delicate, so you are not allowed to visit them. But you can visit another place in southern France where ancient cave paintings were produced. An exact copy of the famous cave at Lascaux was built near the original cave, and the paintings were copied onto the walls. So here, for a short while at least, you can feel like a prehistoric person.

Why don't you try to create your own miniature "cave painting"?
First, take a close look at your favorite pet. Now go outdoors and
find a large, flat rock. After cleaning the rock, use crayons or
paints to make a portrait of your pet on the rock's flat surface.

Horses
c. 30,000 B.C.,
Cave at Chauvet, near
Vallon-Pont-d'Arc

This painting is so
dynamic that it seems as if
the cave artist has painted
the four horses running.
The front animal must
be a foal, or baby horse,
because it is quite
a bit smaller than the
other three.

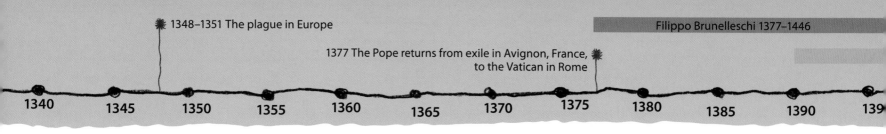

Invention:
The weather is painted realistically for the first time.
Invented by:
Master Wenceslas (died c. 1410 in Trento)
Invented:
c. 1404–1407
Place:
Trento, Italy

Quiz question
Where can you find history's first picture of a snowball?
(Solution on page 46)

La Tempesta (The Tempest)
Giorgione, 1508, Venice, Accademia

In ancient times, people thought you could not draw lightning. The Italian artist Giorgione was the first person who succeeded in painting a flash of lightning.

Weather in Art—The First Painting of a Snowball Fight

Renaissance* painters began to show the weather and the seasons in a way that was true to nature.

Artists, of course, did not discover the weather. And during the Middle Ages, the weather did not interest them either, as most of the stories they painted were about God and the saints. These pictures often showed the sky as a gold or an expensive blue* background. You could almost say that in medieval pictures, the weather and the seasons didn´t exist at all. Painters did not even try to paint nature "accurately." When painting a mountainous landscape, for example, medieval artists didn't even think to look at a proper mountain and try to recreate it as accurately as possible.

After the Middle Ages, however, all that changed. Renaissance* artists began to take an interest once more in ways of painting nature thruthfully. And to help them do that, they "rediscovered" the weather in their paintings, so to speak. One artist even depicted the joys of a winter landscape.

Master Wenceslas lived in about 1400 in a castle in South Tyrol, a mountainous area in what is now northern Italy. In one of the castle's rooms, the bishop for whom he worked wanted him to paint pictures representing the twelve months of the year and the various jobs completed during those months. So Master

8

Stefan Lochner ca. 1410–1452

Masaccio 1401–1428

1453 Constantinople is conquered by the Turks

c. 1390–1441 Jan van Eyck

1400 Italian artist Cennino Cennini publishes the most important textbook on painting in the late Middle Ages

1400 1405 1410 1415 1420 1425 1430 1435 1440 1445 1450 1455

Wenceslas painted people sowing seeds, harvesting crops, picking grapes, chopping down trees, and doing many other things. For January he had a very original idea. Since it is not possible to work in the fields in January, he showed the grand lord and lady of the manor enjoying themselves in the snow. Here, for the very first time in art, Master Wenceslas painted a real snowy landscape. He did not invent the snowball fight, of course, but he was certainly the first person to paint one.

Winter

Master Wenceslas, c. 1404–1407, Trento, Castello del Buonconsiglio, Torre d'Aquila (The Eagle's Tower)

Although the countryside is covered with snow, there is no snow on the castle roofs and there are green bushes growing in the garden. Strangely enough, the man in the garden and the huntsman are bigger than the castle walls. Master Wenceslas had not yet learned the rules of central perspective. You can read about those rules in the next chapter.

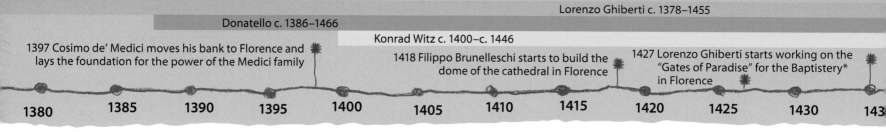

Lorenzo Ghiberti c. 1378–1455

Donatello c. 1386–1466

Konrad Witz c. 1400–c. 1446

1397 Cosimo de' Medici moves his bank to Florence and lays the foundation for the power of the Medici family

1418 Filippo Brunelleschi starts to build the dome of the cathedral in Florence

1427 Lorenzo Ghiberti starts working on the "Gates of Paradise" for the Baptistery* in Florence

1380   1385   1390   1395   1400   1405   1410   1415   1420   1425   1430   143

**La Trinità
(The Trinity)**
Masaccio, c. 1425,
Florence, S. Maria Novella

It was not just the central perspective that was new in Masaccio's fresco; so was the architecture it depicted. The model for this new-looking chapel was probably designed by Masaccio's friend Brunelleschi.

Quiz question
What is the biggest and most famous building by Brunelleschi?
(Solution on page 46)

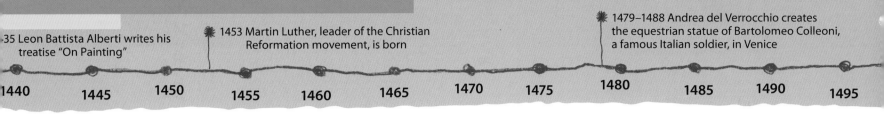

~35 Leon Battista Alberti writes his treatise "On Painting"

✳ 1453 Martin Luther, leader of the Christian Reformation movement, is born

✳ 1479–1488 Andrea del Verrocchio creates the equestrian statue of Bartolomeo Colleoni, a famous Italian soldier, in Venice

1440   1445   1450   1455   1460   1465   1470   1475   1480   1485   1490   1495

Central Perspective— Spaces Become Real

How can you create an impression of depth in a painting so that a picture looks like the real world?

If you look down a long street in a town, you will notice that the houses, the cars, and the people become smaller and smaller the further away they are. And it also looks as if all the straight lines—such as gutters, window ledges, pavements, and streets—are converging on a single point. But how can we represent an impression of depth in a flat picture? And how do we paint the correct proportions in that picture? For hundreds of years these problems were among the most important in art. During the Middle Ages, artists did not yet know how to solve them. That is why a lot of pictures from this time look as if the people are giants or the houses look like crooked little boxes. And you cannot really tell what is at the front of the picture and what is at the back.

Invention:
 Central perspective
Invented by:
 Filippo Brunelleschi
 (born 1377 in Florence,
 died 1446 in Florence)
Invented:
 c. 1420
Place:
 Florence
What is more:
 Brunelleschi also
 built the dome of
 the cathedral in
 Florence.

The solution to this problem was one of the most important inventions in art: it is called central perspective. By using central perspective, it is possible to paint people, roads, and houses and the front and the back of a picture with the right proportions. The man who made this discovery around 1420 was the Italian architect Filippo Brunelleschi. He probably noticed one day, while walking in his hometown of Florence, that the streets seemed to converge in the distance like a series of lines toward a central point. As an architect he had studied geometry, and he started to think about how

**Lo Specchio umano
(The Mirror of Humanity),
fol. 70r**
Domenico Lenzi, 1328–1330,
Florence, Biblioteca Medicea
Laurenziana

In this view of Florence from the Middle Ages, you can see clearly that the buildings do not have a common vanishing point, and the people are far too big for the buildings.

it would be possible to draw a realistic space by using these converging lines. Masaccio, a friend of Brunelleschi, was the first person to try out the new invention properly. In 1425, he painted a chapel with pictures of the Holy Trinity* in the church of Santa Maria Novella in Florence. When the people first saw his fresco* painting in their church, some thought a new chapel had been built. This was because Masaccio had created a perfect illusion, which he achieved by getting the rules of perspective exactly right. The picture's space and the figures painted within it match each other correctly. The Virgin Mary and St. John are shown standing next to Jesus on the Cross, and it looks as if the donors who paid for the painting are kneeling in front of the chapel on the right and left.

The Renaissance* was a period in which science was important and artists discovered how to portray the world as it really was. Brunelleschi's invention was one of the most important steps in this effort. By using central perspective, people could paint what they saw in the right pro-

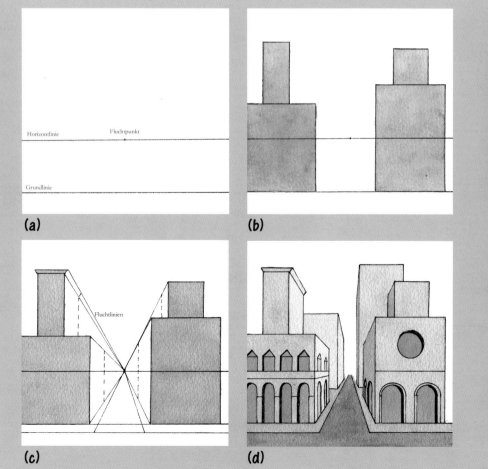

(a)

(b)

(c)

(d)

You can create your own drawing with central perspective

First of all you should draw a base line, where your buildings and people will stand, and a line to represent the horizon, or the height from which you are looking. Then you should mark the vanishing point with a small dot. Draw the front of the buildings on the base line, and then draw lines from the corners of these building fronts to the vanishing point. By using these lines, you can now work out how big a house or some other object will have to be within the picture's space. Try it out!

portions. It was as if the artists had all been waiting for Brunelleschi's idea, because suddenly they all wanted to paint using his method. We still use central perspective today. Architects in particular use it to draw the houses they plan to build.

Over the years, artists invented mechanical devices to help them create perfect perspective in their works. One such invention was called the camera obscura,* a device that led to an even more important creation—photography. But that is another story.

The Triumph of Saint Ignatius
Andrea Pozzo, 1691–1694,
Rome, S. Ignazio

Central perspective was also used in many churches and palaces, sometimes to give the impression of a room which wasn't really there at all. In some churches, when you look at the painted ceiling, it seems as if the space continues upwards and upwards, right up to the sky.

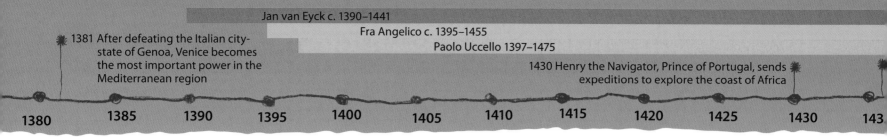
Jan van Eyck c. 1390–1441

Fra Angelico c. 1395–1455

Paolo Uccello 1397–1475

1381 After defeating the Italian city-state of Genoa, Venice becomes the most important power in the Mediterranean region

1430 Henry the Navigator, Prince of Portugal, sends expeditions to explore the coast of Africa

1380   1385   1390   1395   1400   1405   1410   1415   1420   1425   1430   143

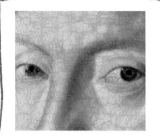

Invention:
  Self-portrait
Invented by:
  Jan van Eyck
  (born c. 1390 in
  Maaseik, died
  1441 in Bruges)
Invented:
  1433
Place:
  Bruges
What is more:
  Jan van Eyck
  painted himself
  with a fancy
  turban.

Why not paint your own self-portrait!
Just position yourself in front of a mirror and try it out. If you use two mirrors and position them at an angle, you can also paint yourself in profile.

The Self-Portrait—Artists Look at Themselves in the Mirror

During the Renaissance,* artists gained a new self-confidence and started to make themselves the subject of their pictures.

One of the many jobs of painters was to create pictures of important people—portraits of the mayor, the prince, or the bishop. City leaders would often choose the best artist for this task.

Jan van Eyck was the best artist in his hometown of Bruges. He was one of the first to paint with oil paints,* which gave his pictures especially bright colors and an unusual brilliance. Van Eyck's paintings were so famous, they were talked about all over Europe.

One day, Jan van Eyck decided that he would like to have a picture of himself. And since he was the best artist in town, he simply decided to paint his own portrait. This seemed like a strange decision to people in Bruges. Until van Eyck's day, painters were regarded only as good craftsmen—certainly not important enough to be the subjects of paintings.

So van Eyck sat down in front of a mirror, looked at himself carefully, and painted his face exactly as he saw it. The picture is very small (the head is only about 8 cm in height), and yet we can even see the stubble of his beard. In order to make it clear to everyone that he really had painted the picture himself, he wrote on the frame, "Jan van Eyck made me in 1433, 21 October". It is a remarkable portrait, made even more striking by the beautiful red turban on the artist's head.

14

Portrait of a Man in a Turban (Self-Portrait)
Jan van Eyck, 1433, London, National Gallery

By using oil paint, Jan van Eyck could depict his face so finely that we can see all the little wrinkles. And you can almost feel how soft and fluffy the fur collar on his coat is.

Self-Portrait at the age of Thirteen
Albrecht Dürer, 1484,
drawing, Vienna,
Albertina

For this drawing Dürer
used a silverpoint
stylus,* which was what
artists employed in
those days instead of
a pencil. Albrecht later
wrote in the top corner:
"I drew this picture of
myself by looking in a
mirror in 1484, when I
was still a child."

After van Eyck, many other artists also started painting portraits of themselves. Sometimes they tried pulling funny faces or using special lighting effects; or they decided to show themselves in certain situations in life, when they were either very happy or very sad.

The young Albrecht Dürer was a special case. When he was twelve years old he became an apprentice to his father, who was a goldsmith. But Albrecht really wanted to become a painter. So he spent a lot of time drawing and became very good at it. The picture on the left is the first one we have by him, and it is a self-portrait. We can see young Albrecht looking very attentively towards his right, in the direction that his finger is pointing. He was probably staring at the mirror that he used to create the portrait. And so the hand that we can see is not his right hand, but his left one. He was using his right hand to draw his portrait.

Four Self-Portraits
Rembrandt, 1630, engravings,
J. de Bruijn Collection

The Dutch artist Rembrandt van Rijn drew himself with various expressions on his face. Sometimes he looks amazed, sometimes he is laughing, and other times he looks serious or seems to be cross.

**Martyrdom of the Ten Thousand Christians
(Detail with Self-Portrait of Albrecht Dürer)**
Albrecht Dürer, 1508, Vienna,
Kunsthistorisches Museum

Albrecht Dürer liked to include himself in his pictures. Here he showed himself holding up a shield, on which he wrote that he was the artist who painted the picture.

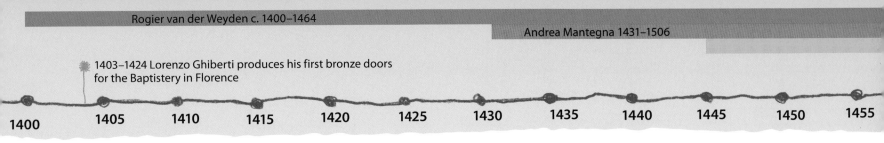

Invention:
First painting of
a real landscape

Invented by:
Konrad Witz (born
1400 in Rottweil am
Neckar, died 1445
in Geneva)

Invented:
1444

Place:
Geneva

What is more:
Although Geneva
was not usually a
city where artistic
progress took place,
Konrad Witz was
certainly up to
date.

Landscape Painting—Bible Stories Outside Our Front Door

The Swiss artist Konrad Witz was one of the most innovative artists of his time.

The citizens of Geneva must have been very surprised indeed when, in 1444, they first saw the painting *The Miraculous Draught of Fishes* in the Cathedral of St. Peter. This remarkable artwork showed a realistic image of the city's own lake, Lake Geneva. It was something completely new. Konrad Witz, the painter of the picture, had actually used a real landscape as the setting for a Bible story.

In the Middle Ages, the stories that artists painted nearly always came from the Bible. Since these stories took place far away and a long time ago, the artists saw no reason to paint real landscapes. And because very few people could read or write, the Bible stories had to be told in pictures which were as simple as possible. The picture on the left tells the same story as the picture by Konrad Witz – but look how different it is! For the medieval artist it was sufficient to paint a few wavy lines, and everyone knew that he wanted us to imagine a lake.

**Codex Aureus Epternacensis,
The Miraculous Draught of Fishes**
c. 1030, Nuremberg,
Germanisches Nationalmuseum

Although the lake and other features of this picture are painted simply, we can recognize all the things that are important for the story. Such paintings were a great achievement of medieval art.

But in Konrad Witz's time, in the Renaissance,* artists began to take an interest in nature and how it could be

The Miraculous Draught of Fishes
Konrad Witz, 1444, Geneva, Musée d'art et d'histoire

The idea of setting a Bible story in a real landscape was a new invention in painting. By doing so, Konrad Witz made people realize that the stories in the Bible are important for everyone, no matter where they live.

portrayed. The story which Witz is telling us in his picture is the one where Jesus calls upon St. Peter to follow Him. That took place on the Sea of Galilee, which, as everyone knows, is not in Switzerland. Nonetheless, Witz tried to show what the story might have looked like had it happened in his own country. The people recognized the landscape that they saw every day: the stilted dwellings by the lake, the houses and castles, and the

View of Arco
Albrecht Dürer, 1495, Paris, Louvre

This is what it looked like when young Albrecht painted his watercolor …

snow-capped mountain peak of Mont Blanc in the background.

Other Renaissance artists began to make landscape paintings without people in it. They created these pictures not to portray Bible stories, but simply because the landscapes were beautiful or interesting. Albrecht Dürer was one such artist. When he traveled to Italy in 1494, he drew pictures of the most important places he visited. Whenever he had time, he took some paper and his paints and painted whatever interested him. By doing this, Dürer helped invent the holiday picture.

Why don't you create some landscape pictures on holiday? But paint them yourself, don't just photograph them!

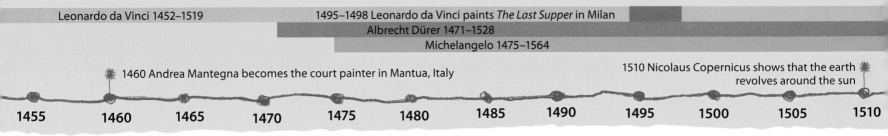

Leonardo da Vinci 1452–1519

1495–1498 Leonardo da Vinci paints *The Last Supper* in Milan

Albrecht Dürer 1471–1528

Michelangelo 1475–1564

★ 1460 Andrea Mantegna becomes the court painter in Mantua, Italy

1510 Nicolaus Copernicus shows that the earth ★
revolves around the sun

1455   1460   1465   1470   1475   1480   1485   1490   1495   1500   1505   1510

Invention:
Copperplate engraving

Invented by:
We do not know who really discovered it. It developed from the work of armorers and goldsmiths.

Discovered:
Around 1430/1440

Place:
The first copperplate engravings were probably made in the Upper Rhine region of Germany.

What is more:
Copperplate engravings enabled artists to be much more precise than they could be with woodcuts. They could also make many more prints from the same plate.

Quiz question
How long did Dürer need to make his copperplate engraving *Knight, Death and the Devil?*

(Solution on page 46)

Copperplate Engraving— The Beginnings of Mass Media

In earlier times, in the days before the Internet, how did artists and their works become famous? How could people find out how other artists worked?

Today it's no problem to upload our own paintings or photographs onto the Internet. When we do this, anybody who is interested in them can see them, anywhere in the world. In earlier times, however, seeing art wasn't so easy. Once an artist had finished a picture, it was usually put on display in a church, in a castle, or in the home of the person who had commissioned it. Anyone who wanted to see it had to travel to the place where the picture was on show. But what did artists do if they wanted to advertise themselves or their pictures? Or if they wanted to know what their fellow artists in other countries were painting? For them, it was a stroke of luck that the copperplate engraving was invented in the fifteenth century. And the idea for this invention, like so many others in the history of art, came from a field outside of art. The idea for copperplate engraving came from the armorers, who used engravings to make decorative patterns on valuable weapons and armor.

Artists developed the idea further. They scratched their drawings onto copper plates, coated them with paint so that all the indentations were filled with color, and then pressed them onto damp paper. This type of process is called intaglio printing.* In this way they could make copies of their drawings and paintings and then sell them. But they did not have to make a new drawing or painting each time, which of course would have taken them much longer. The artists could print the copper engraving time and time again and sell it on the market or send it to someone. This was how artistic ideas spread

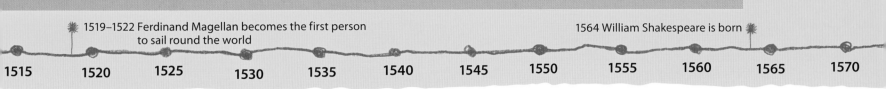

Knight, Death and the Devil
Albrecht Dürer, 1513,
copperplate engraving

Beside the proud knight, Death is riding along on an old nag with his hourglass in his hand. Behind the horse, we can see an evil-looking Devil with his cloven hoof, which frightens even the dog.

Did you know?
One of the most important inventions for art is so obvious that we might overlook it: paper. The Chinese already had paper 2,000 years ago, but it did not reach Europe until the 1100s. Before that time, artists drew on tanned animal skins, which were known as parchment. The first paper mill was built in Italy in 1276, and in 1390 the first paper mill in Germany was built in Nuremberg. And from that point onwards, paper began to replace parchment, which was much more expensive.

across the whole of Europe. For example, an Italian painter could now know what his colleagues in Germany or England were painting.

One of the most famous artists who made copperplate engravings was Albrecht Dürer from Nuremberg, Germany. His copperplate engravings were so well-known and popular that the Italian engraver Marcantonio Raimondi copied the engravings and sold them as originals.

William Blake 1757–1827

Katsushika Hokusai 1760–1849

William Turner 1775–1851

1756 Austrian composer Wolfgang
Amadeus Mozart is born

1776 Declaration of Independence
of the United States of America

1789 French Revolution

1798 German inventor
Alois Senefelder
develops lithogra

1750　　1755　　1760　　1765　　1770　　1775　　1780　　1785　　1790　　1795　　1800　　180

View from a window in Le Gras
Nicéphore Niépce, 1827, University of Texas,
Gernsheim Collection

At the very beginning of photography, exposure
times were too long to take portraits of people.
So the earliest photographs depicted only buildings
and still lifes.

1817 German inventor Karl Freiherr Drais von Sauerbronn develops the velocipede, an early type of bicycle

1848 Karl Marx and Friedrich Engels publish the "Communist Manifesto," the founding document of the Communist political philosophy

| 1810 | 1815 | 1820 | 1825 | 1830 | 1835 | 1840 | 1845 | 1850 | 1855 | 1860 | 1865 |

Photography—Pictures Without Paint or Paintbrush

The first photograph ever taken was a rather blurry view of a backyard. It was created by Nicéphore Niépce in 1827 in France.

Invention:
  Photography
Inventor:
  Nicéphore Niépce
  (b. 1765 in Chalon-sur-Saône, d. 1833 in Saint-Loup-de-Varennes)
Created:
  1827
Place:
  Saint-Loup-de-Varennes
What is more:
  In 1798, Niépce and his brother Claude developed an internal combustion engine with which they could power a boat.

Cameras have actually been around for much longer than photography. In order to make reproductions of their surroundings that were as accurate as possible, artists hundreds of years ago used something called a camera obscura.* Using a camera obscura, a picture is projected through a lens onto a pane of glass and can then be copied by hand and transferred onto a large canvas.

But in the early 1800s, people began to wonder if they could create a picture that did not need to be drawn by hand at all; a picture that would draw itself, so to speak. The camera existed already, and people had also known for a long time that there were substances that were sensitive to light. Now, all that they had to do was to bring these two ideas together to create an "automatic drawing." In 1827, the time had come at last. French inventor Nicéphore Niépce positioned the camera he had built at a window on the first floor of his house, and he "clicked" for the first time. This "click" lasted eight hours, however, because that is how long Niépce had to expose the world's first photograph until it was finished. Niépce still referred to it as "heliography" ("sun writing"), however, because it was actually the sun that had made his photograph. The term "photograph" ("writing with light") was coined by the English inventor Sir John Herschel.

Louis Daguerre developed his colleague Niépce's invention further. Although Niépce had invented photography, it was Daguerre who

Delage Automobil
Jacques Henri Lartigue, 1912

Lartigue was just 18 years old when he took this photograph. He was one of the first people to take snapshots. Here he managed to take an unusual picture of a race car zooming past him. Lartigue moved the camera alongside the car as it raced on by. Because of the speed of the car—and the speed of Lartigue's camera shutter—the car's wheels have an elliptical shape in the photo.

improved it to the extent that it could be used by anyone. In 1839, he sold a book in which he explained his method and included construction plans for a camera.

Although the invention of photography was a great success, making photographs remained a very laborious process because the exposure time was still several minutes long. Developing the pictures was very complicated too. But these problems were solved at the beginning of the twentieth century. Cameras became simpler and film became more light-sensitive, so that you could take snapshots like the photograph above by Jacques Henri Lartigue. Now everybody could have a go at being a photographer. Film was sent off to be developed and the finished photographs were sent back.

But what did painters do after photography had been invented in 1827? Some of them became photographers themselves, and others used photography for their painting. Many painters, including the famous French artists Eugène Delacroix and Edgar Degas, often didn't make sketches anymore, but used photographs as the models from which they painted. German artist Franz von Lenbach's family portraits show this process very clearly. He photographed himself with his family, and then he painted the picture in color. This made it much easier for him to create the right composition and the proper expressions on the people's faces.

Photography was important for painting in another way, too. Before the photograph, recreating nature as accurately as possible was a key function of painting. Photography could achieve this function more easily and more successfully, giving painters the freedom to focus on other things in their art instead. Artists started to express their feelings in their paintings; and color, which did not yet play a role in the photography of the time, became increasingly important in painting.

Since the invention of digital photography, the use of film for photographs has decreased. The first digital camera was developed in 1975. It weighed 4 kilograms, or 9 pounds, and needed 23 seconds to make one small picture! That's hard to believe when most cell phones nowadays have cameras that produce photographs of a much higher quality.

Family portrait
Franz von Lenbach, 1903, photograph and painting, Munich, Städtische Galerie im Lenbachhaus

Lenbach's daughter on the right-hand side looks a bit grumpy in the photograph. In his painting, the artist has managed to conjure a little smile onto her face.

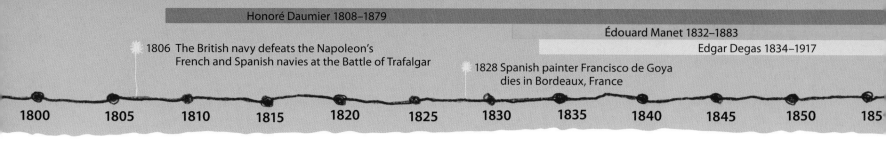

Honoré Daumier 1808–1879

Édouard Manet 1832–1883

Edgar Degas 1834–1917

1806 The British navy defeats the Napoleon's
French and Spanish navies at the Battle of Trafalgar

1828 Spanish painter Francisco de Goya
dies in Bordeaux, France

| 1800 | 1805 | 1810 | 1815 | 1820 | 1825 | 1830 | 1835 | 1840 | 1845 | 1850 | 185 |

Invention:
Paint tube
Inventor:
John Goffe Rand
(b. 1801 in Bedford,
New Hampshire,
d. 1873 in New York)
Created:
1841
Place:
London

The Paint Tube—
Out of the Studio!

Sometimes very small things have enormous consequences. One example is an invention by the American painter John Rand, which changed art more than he could possibly have imagined.

Annoyed that his paint always dried out when he was painting outside, John Rand decided to fill the paint into little zinc tubes. In this way, he invented the paint tube in 1841. Now he could transport his paint easily, and he could close the tubes when he wasn't using them. Until then, paint had been transported in bags made of animal bladders, which could not be closed again once they had been opened. This meant that the paint dried out quickly and couldn't be used anymore.

The invention of the paint tube was particularly appealing to a group of young artists in France. Among them were painters who are now famous, like Claude Monet, Auguste Renoir, and many others. They didn't want to be restricted to painting in their studios anymore. They wanted to be outdoors, to capture the light and colors of nature in their paintings.

One morning in 1872, Claude Monet went off to the port of Le Havre and painted the sunrise there. He gave his picture the title *Impression, Sunrise*. Looking at the painting, you almost feel as though you were gazing at the scene yourself—but with blurred vision.

When this painting and others by the young group of painters were first exhibited in Paris in 1874, they created a great commotion. The critics got really worked up about the paintings, which didn't seem to have the precise,

1863 The first under-
ground train starts
running in London

1872 American inventor Thomas
Adams develops chewing gum

1885 German manufacturer Carl Benz constructs the first car with a gas engine
1908 Georges Braque and Pablo Picasso develop the Cubist style of painting

1860　1865　1870　1875　1880　1885　1890　1895　1900　1905　1910　1915

Impression, Sunrise
Claude Monet, 1872, Paris, Musée Marmottan

Originally, the painting was just called *Lake Landscape*. But this title was too boring for the exhibition of 1874.
And so Monet decided to call it *Impression, Sunrise*, simultaneously naming a new artistic movement: Impressionism.

Claude Monet and his Wife on the Studio Boat
Édouard Manet, 1874, Munich, Neue Pinakothek

Claude Monet had a studio boat specially made so that he could paint on the river Seine.

realistic detail that was the customary in art at the time. But Monet did not want to make paintings like that, he just wanted to capture the spontaneous impression of a sunrise. And he could do that best by painting it onto the canvas quickly, rather than trying to capture all the precise detail.

Because of the angry reaction that this particular painting received from a critic, the young painters decided to call themselves "Impressionists" at their next exhibition. The new name sounded good, and the artists also wanted to annoy that critic a little bit.

But it was not just the way these artists painted that was new: what they painted was new as well. Until then, the subjects of paintings were usually from the Bible or from stories about mighty rulers. These stories didn't interest the Impressionists at all, however. They wanted to depict nature and the lives of ordinary people: how they danced, went for walks, or sat in cafés. These new subjects for painting bothered nineteenth century viewers even more than the casual way in which the Impressionists had painted them.

It took a few years before people got used to Impressionism, and before the art became popular. Until then, the Impressionists sold only a small number of paintings. Nowadays, however, the artworks of Claude Monet and his friends are among the most expensive in the world.

The Impressionists revolutionized art, thanks in part to their colleague John Rand and his small, but important, invention of the paint tube.

Dance at Le Moulin de la Galette
Auguste Renoir, 1876, Paris, Musée d'Orsay

"Leisure" was a completely new subject in painting. These sorts of scenes are typical of the Impressionists, who were not interested in stories about rulers. The bright, cheerful atmosphere of the images' soft light is another important feature of Impressionist painting.

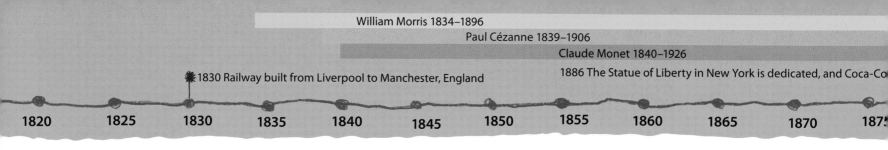

William Morris 1834–1896

Paul Cézanne 1839–1906

Claude Monet 1840–1926

1830 Railway built from Liverpool to Manchester, England

1886 The Statue of Liberty in New York is dedicated, and Coca-Co

| 1820 | 1825 | 1830 | 1835 | 1840 | 1845 | 1850 | 1855 | 1860 | 1865 | 1870 | 1875 |

Invention:
The cartoon

Inventor:
Wilhelm Busch (b. 1832 in Wiedensahl, d. 1908 in Mechtshausen), Rudolph Dirks (b. 1877 in Heide, d. 1968 in New York) and many others

Created:
Middle to end of the 19th century

Places:
Munich and New York

What is more:
To differentiate strip cartoons from other types of picture stories that have existed in art, the cartoons are also known as "sequential art."

The Virtuouso, Finale furioso
Wilhelm Busch, 1865

Looking at this picture of a pianist, one can just about hear how wildly and quickly he hammers down the piano keys. The listener's ears swell up and the notes tumble out of the piano. Such forms of representation did not exist before Wilhelm Busch.

The Cartoon—
Pictures Learn to Speak

Picture stories were the forerunners of cartoons. Cartoons as we know them today first came from the United States, where little picture stories were published in newspapers at the end of the nineteenth century.

Sometimes it isn't easy to say who invented something, because different people in different places come up with similar ideas. This applies to cartoons, too. The cartoon series "The Katzenjammer Kids" was first printed in an American newspaper called the *New York Journal* on December 12, 1897. This was one of the first cartoons, and it was created by Rudolph Dirks, who had moved from Germany to America. The twins Hans and Fritz are the main characters, and they constantly play tricks on their mother and other people around them. But these characters were modeled on earlier ones called Max and Moritz, who were invented by German illustrator Wilhelm Busch in 1865. Max and Moritz had already become world famous. Their stories were translated into English in 1870, and in 1887 they were even translated into Japanese. Rudolph Dirks just adopted the idea from Wilhelm Busch and turned it into a cartoon series, which is still printed in American newspapers today.

Summer No. 13
Title page
Rudolph Dirks

The language of the Katzenjammer Kids is a strange combination of English and German. This is because a lot of immigrants from Germany lived in New York at this time.

The Katzenjammer Kids collect stray Cats and hide them in Mamma's room
Rudolph Dirks, *The New York Journal,* 5.6.1898, Hannover, Wilhelm-Busch-Museum

Hans and Fritz look very similar to the comic characters after which they were modeled. And just like Max and Moritz, they play naughty tricks and are always punished for them.

What was new about cartoons was the way in which they told stories. Each picture had its own frame, known as a "panel," and the characters usually spoke in speech bubbles. The form of representation was new, too. So-called "speed lines" were used to show the movement of objects or figures in cartoons. Another way of showing movement was to depict the same object (a hand, for example) in different positions at the same time. Wilhelm Busch had already come up with that idea before cartoons were created in the United States. He is therefore the father, or at least the grandfather, of cartoon art.

Another particularity of cartoons is the use of onomatopoeia—or words that sound like what they mean. Such words occur rarely in art before the 1900s. It would probably look weird if there were a **wham!** or a **pow!** in a painting of a saint.

Quiz question
What is the most expensive cartoon in the world?
(Answer on page 46)

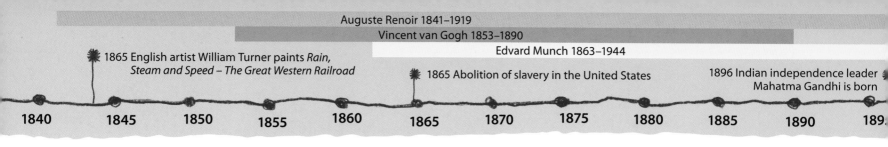

Auguste Renoir 1841–1919
Vincent van Gogh 1853–1890

Edvard Munch 1863–1944

1865 English artist William Turner paints *Rain, Steam and Speed – The Great Western Railroad*

1865 Abolition of slavery in the United States

1896 Indian independence leader Mahatma Gandhi is born

1840　1845　1850　1855　1860　1865　1870　1875　1880　1885　1890　189.

White Forms
Franz Kline, 1955,
New York,
Museum of Modern Art

Because an abstract painting doesn't represent anything in the real world, it is sometimes helpful to look at the work's title. Franz Kline created a painting on which, at first glance, you just see black stripes on a white canvas. But the painting is called "White Forms." If you look at the image again, paying attention to the "white" forms, it appears to be the other way around: white shapes on a black background.

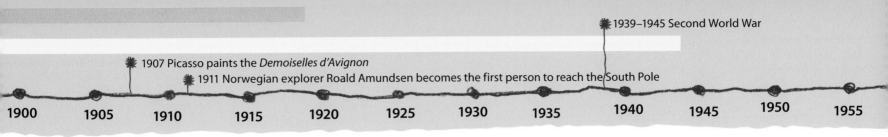

* 1939–1945 Second World War

* 1907 Picasso paints the *Demoiselles d'Avignon*
* 1911 Norwegian explorer Roald Amundsen becomes the first person to reach the South Pole

1900　**1905**　**1910**　**1915**　**1920**　**1925**　**1930**　**1935**　**1940**　**1945**　**1950**　**1955**

Abstract Art— Feelings Turn Into Paintings

How can paintings arouse feelings similar to those conjured up in music?

You must know what it's like: listening to a particular piece of music, you suddenly feel happy or sad. It's like that for most people. Music arouses feelings or moods. Wassily Kandinsky wanted to achieve that with his paintings, too. He felt that the painting of his time was not "musical" enough, and he wanted to find new forms of expression for his art— forms that would appeal to people's feelings as directly as music. But Kandinsky didn't know how to achieve this. So he searched for a new type of art, traveling from his home city of Moscow to Paris. There, he met painters such as Henri Matisse and Georges Braque, who used color in new and exciting ways. Kandinsky also got to know the painting of

Invention:
　Abstract painting
Inventor:
　Wassily Kandinsky
　(b. 1866 in Moscow,
　d. 1944 in Neuilly-
　sur-Seine)
Place:
　Munich

Black Square
Kazimir Malevich, 1915,
Moscow, Tretyakov State
Gallery

Russian painter Kazimir Malevich created some of the most radical abstract art of the early 1900s. His paintings often feature nothing but simple shapes. This work shows only a black square on a white background.

the Impressionists. After leaving Paris, he went to Munich and got together with Franz Marc and other painters. These young artists established a famous group called the "Blauer Reiter," which means "Blue Rider."

Kandinsky got to know many artists and their paintings, spent lots of time thinking, and tried out new methods of making art. Still, however, he had not achieved what he wanted to achieve. Sometimes, even a great artist needs some luck in order to come up with a new invention. One evening, he went into his studio and noticed a painting in the corner. Kandinsky was convinced that he had not seen it before, but he thought it was great. He couldn't actually make out a landscape or objects in the painting, only colors and shapes. And that is when the idea struck him: if he wanted to express his feelings, he didn't have to paint objects, but rather shapes and colors. This sort of art became known as "abstract art." Kandinsky went on to paint the first abstract watercolors.

The following day, Wassily noticed that the painting which had caught his eye the previous evening was actually one of his own. It just happened to be upside down.

You may wonder why Kandinsky's first abstract artworks were watercolors and not paintings. Kandinsky probably wanted to experiment with his new idea, so he created small watercolors before making full-sized abstract paintings. At the beginning of the twentieth century, it was virtually unthinkable to paint pictures in which nothing could be recognized. An artist who did so would have been called an impostor and a bungler.

Nowadays, abstract painting is not unusual anymore. Artists worldwide use abstract shapes to show us their feelings or to create feelings in us, as Kandinsky did. When we look at an abstract painting, we cannot see anything specific, but we can learn a great deal about how we look at art and the world.

Untitled
Wassily Kandinsky, 1910, watercolor, Paris, Centre Pompidou,
Musée National d'Art Moderne

Looking at this painting, it really isn't possible to identify
anything specific. The picture consists of nothing but abstract
shapes and colors. In 1912, Kandinsky wrote a book about his
artistic ideas and called it *About the Spiritual in Art*.

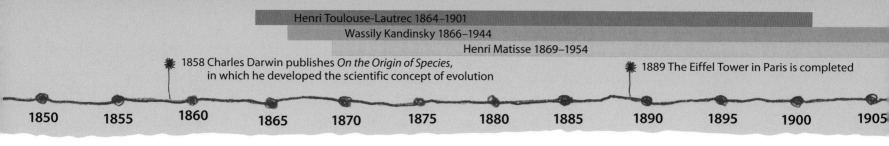

Henri Toulouse-Lautrec 1864–1901
Wassily Kandinsky 1866–1944
Henri Matisse 1869–1954

1858 Charles Darwin publishes *On the Origin of Species*, in which he developed the scientific concept of evolution

1889 The Eiffel Tower in Paris is completed

1850 1855 1860 1865 1870 1875 1880 1885 1890 1895 1900 1905

Invention:
Readymades, or ready-made objects, declared to be art

Inventor:
Marcel Duchamp (b. 1887 in Blainville-Crevon, d. 1968 in Neuilly-sur-Seine)

Created:
1913

Place:
Paris

What is more:
Duchamp signed a number of ready-mades using a different name. He signed the urinal with the name "R. Mutt," for example.

The Readymade— Everyday Objects in Art

How is art created without the artist lifting a paintbrush?

Is everything an artist does really art? Most people would probably answer "yes." For example, a landscape painted by Albrecht Dürer is art, just as a self-portrait by Vincent van Gogh is art. This was also true of Marcel Duchamp. He painted lots of pictures and showed them in exhibitions in France and in the United States. But when it came to the question of whether everything an artist does is art, Duchamp went one step further. One day, he took the rim of an ordinary bicycle tire, mounted it on a stool, and simply declared it to be art.

He did the same thing with various other objects. For example, he took an ordinary urinal, such as one might find in any lavatory (it was, of course, unused), and signed it with a name not his own. Again he declared that this object was now art.

Fountain
Marcel Duchamp, 1917, London, Tate Modern

As with *Bicycle Wheel*, the original of the urinal does not exist anymore. But there are replicas of this work in many museums. Duchamp even created a few miniature versions of it.

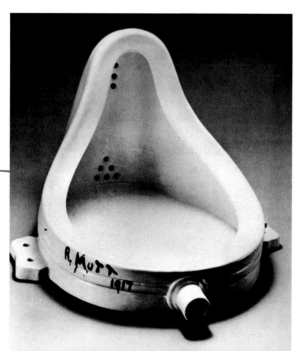

At first, this way of "making" art sounded quite strange, and lots of people became angry when Duchamp's works were considered art. But of course, Marcel Duchamp had done it for a reason. By taking everyday objects and exhibiting them outside their usual contexts, he drew people's attention to the perfect form of those objects. And when he, as an artist, selected one of the objects and put it on a

38

1948 The Universal Declaration of Human Rights is adopted by the United Nations General Assembly

1913 The Armory Show, which helped bring modern art to the United States, takes place in New York City | 1961 Construction of the Berlin Wall
1925 The Leica, the first miniature camera, comes on the market

1910   1915   1920   1925   1930   1935   1940   1945   1950   1955   1960   1965

pedestal (so to speak), it became an artwork. Such artworks are called "readymades" precisely because the artist does not create anything himself or herself. For Duchamp, this was an important artistic idea.

As you will have noticed by reading this book, artists sometimes achieve quick success by doing particular things at particular times. At other times, however, an artist's invention provokes strong protests from audiences and critics. Readymades are an example of an art form that struggled at first and was only accepted gradually by viewers as time went by. Nowadays, there are lots of artists who use everyday objects for their artworks. The audiences are no longer as annoyed by this type of art as they were during Duchamp's time.

Did you know?
Marcel Duchamp was an enthusiastic chess player and even a member of the French national chess team. He took part in five chess Olympiads between 1924 and 1933.

Bicycle Wheel
Marcel Duchamp, 1951 (third replica after the original lost in 1913), New York, Museum of Modern Art

The original Bicycle Wheel has, sadly, been lost. There is just one photograph of it. It is said that Duchamp's sister Suzanne threw it away because she thought it was junk.

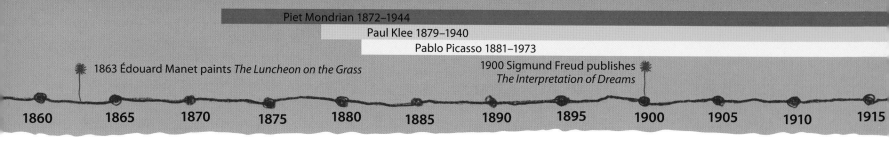

Piet Mondrian 1872–1944
Paul Klee 1879–1940
Pablo Picasso 1881–1973

1863 Édouard Manet paints *The Luncheon on the Grass*

1900 Sigmund Freud publishes *The Interpretation of Dreams*

1860　1865　1870　1875　1880　1885　1890　1895　1900　1905　1910　1915

Invention:
Action painting, drip painting

Inventor:
Jackson Pollock (b. 1912 in Cody, Wyoming, d. 1956 in East Hampton, New York)

Created:
1947

Place:
New York

What is more:
The photographer Hans Namuth often took photographs of Pollock in the process of painting. These photographs have become almost as famous as Pollock's artwork.

Did you know?
A critic said about Pollock's art that the paintings were ugly, but that "all thoroughly original art looks horrible at first glance."

Action Painting—Splashy Art

The art of painting was revolutionized by Impressionism and abstract art. What did the artists do with their new-found freedom?

Is a painting still art if one can't recognize anything in it? Of course it is, because art does not have to reproduce the real world precisely. In earlier times, however, artists did have to make art this way. The person who could paint things in the most natural manner was considered to be the best painter. These days, photography does that job, and the point of art is now more about expressing one's feelings or provoking feelings in the viewer. And it was for this purpose that the American painter Jackson Pollock invented an entirely new way of painting. It is known as "action painting" or "drip painting." Pollock would place one of his gigantic canvases on the floor, make holes in his paint cans, and let the paint "drip" onto the canvas.

Jackson Pollock in the process of painting
Hans Namuth, photograph, New York, Pollock Krasner Foundation

Pollock placed his gigantic canvases on the floor and splashed paint on them. Sometimes, it looked as though he was dancing around the canvas when he painted.

1947 American scientist Edwin Land develops the instant camera

1939–1945 Second World War

1937 Picasso paints *Guernica*

1949 Establishment of the Federal Republic of Germany

1953 Mount Everest, the tallest mountain in the world, is climbed for the first time

| 1920 | 1925 | 1930 | 1935 | 1940 | 1945 | 1950 | 1955 | 1960 | 1965 | 1970 | 1975 |

Number 1A
Jackson Pollock, 1948,
New York, Museum of
Modern Art

Pollock's paintings appear not to have a beginning or an end. You can't make out anything except for a tight network of lines and drips. Pollock was also known as "Jack the Dripper" because of his drip paintings.

Sometimes, this artist would use a paintbrush to splash the paint onto the canvas, and then work on it with sticks or palette knives. Pollock did not paint a particular subject, such as a landscape, a portrait, or a story. He gave free rein to his temperament and just painted what he felt. The paintings were different every time, depending on whether he was sad, happy, or angry. For him, the most important thing was not the finished painting, but the process of painting itself.

When Pollock created a painting, it was almost as though he was dancing on and around the canvas. He looked quite wild when he painted. I'll bet you haven't painted like that at school! What Pollock created in this way looks, at first glance, like a mess of lines, blotches, and drips. But if you spend a little bit longer looking at the images, you can see a rhythm and a power that make Pollock's paintings great art.

You can create your own drip painting on this website: www.jacksonpollock.org.

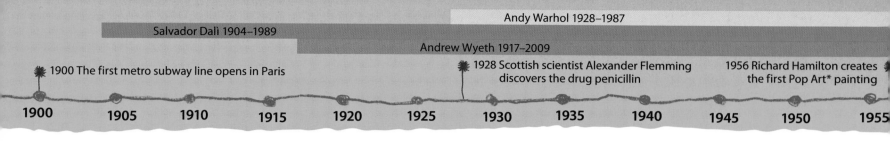

Salvador Dalì 1904–1989

Andy Warhol 1928–1987

Andrew Wyeth 1917–2009

1900 The first metro subway line opens in Paris

1928 Scottish scientist Alexander Flemming discovers the drug penicillin

1956 Richard Hamilton creates the first Pop Art* painting

| 1900 | 1905 | 1910 | 1915 | 1920 | 1925 | 1930 | 1935 | 1940 | 1945 | 1950 | 1955 |

Invention:
Aerosol spray can
Inventor:
Erik Rotheim
(b. 1898 in Kristiania,
d. 1938 in Oslo)
Creation:
1926
Place:
Oslo

Graffiti— The City as Canvas

The word "graffiti" comes from the Greek word "graphein", and it means "to write." In the ancient world, people were already painting or scratching political slogans onto walls.

Graffiti is a modern form of art. Lots of artists, and young artists in particular, don't want to make art only in their studios, painting one canvas after the other. They go outside and spray their pictures onto the walls of the city.

Graffiti art was made possible, in large part, through an invention by Norwegian scientist Erik Rotheim. In 1926, he invented the spray can, which makes it possible to spray large surfaces easily and very quickly. What tubes of paint were to the Impressionists, spray cans are to graffiti artists.

There are, however, two problems that hamper this young art form. First, spraying anything onto the walls of buildings is usually against the law. So many sprayers prefer to remain anonymous in order to avoid being punished. Second, lots of graffiti consists only of ugly scribbles. Luckily there are some real artists among the sprayers, and they spray against graffiti's negative image. Thanks to them, this art form is gaining increasing recognition. One of the first grafitti artists called himself the "Sprayer of Zurich" (his real name is Harald Naegeli), because he sprayed more than 400 figures, such as *Undine*, onto the buildings of Zurich, Switzerland between 1977 and 1979. Naegeli had to go to prison for nine months when he was caught in 1984. Nowadays, he is successful as a true artist.

Untitled
Banksy, 2007, Bethlehem

Banksy made this dove of peace in Bethlehem in 2007 to protest against the 25-kilometer-long concrete wall that separates the Palestinian territories from Israel.

42

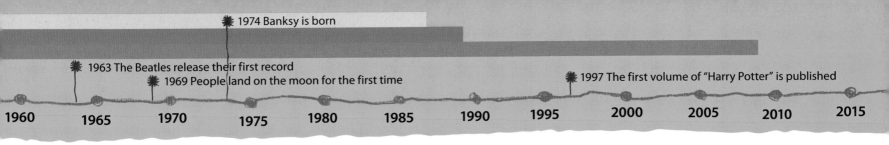

* 1974 Banksy is born

* 1963 The Beatles release their first record
* 1969 People land on the moon for the first time   * 1997 The first volume of "Harry Potter" is published

1960   1965   1970   1975   1980   1985   1990   1995   2000   2005   2010   2015

The Englishman Banksy is one of the most famous graffiti artists. His graffiti can be found in many different cities throughout the world. But hardly anybody knows who he is. And those who do know won't tell. Banksy creates works that make people think: for example, he portrays the dove of peace wearing a warlike, bulletproof vest. Some of his graffiti, on the other hand, is funny: a zebra whose stripes have just been washed off, for example. Banksy uses the so-called stencil technique. This involves cutting the different parts of the picture out of a piece of cardboard and then spraying them onto walls.

Although people have not yet worked out who Banksy really is, his work is shown in popular exhibitions and sells for very high prices. Because his artwork is of such high quality, Banksy has greatly increased the esteem in which graffiti art is held.

And Banksy's success is thanks, in part, to Eric Rotheim, the inventor of spray cans. Rotheim could hardly have imagined that his invention would lead to the creation of a new art form.

Undine
Harald Naegeli, 1978, Zurich

Harald Naegeli was severely punished for this and similar graffiti. In 1995, *Undine* was declared to be worth preserving, and Naegeli was acknowledged as an artist. The artwork was restored in 2004.

Did you know?
In 2010, Banksy made a pretty cool film about graffiti: *Exit through the Gift Shop*. But even here you won't recognize Banksy, for he is sitting in the dark and has pulled a hood down over his face.

Tip On this website you will find a list of walls all over the world on which you can spray graffiti legally: http://www.legal-walls.net

Glossary

CAMERA OBSCURA This boxlike device, which was given the Latin name for "dark room," was once used as a drawing aid. It works somewhat like a camera does. The object you want to draw is projected through a lens onto a pane of glass so that you can easily copy it. The principle of the camera obscura was known as far back as antiquity. From the Renaissance* to the invention of photography, many artists used camera obscuras for their paintings.

FRESCO A fresco is a painting that is made on the wet plaster on a wall. Once it has dried, the paint and the wall are fused together, so that the artwork cannot peel off so easily. Because of the way they are made, these paintings can last a long time.

HOLY TRINITY In Christianity, the "Trinity" refers to the unity of God the Father, his Son Jesus, and the Holy Spirit, which is often represented as a dove.

PRECIOUS BLUE The blue in many old book illustrations and paintings was made from the semi-precious stone called lapis lazuli. This stone came primarily from Afghanistan and was once considered as precious as gold. Because the stone had to travel such a long way to reach Europe, Europeans also called the stone ultramarine (Latin for "beyond the sea").

OIL PAINT To make oil paint, color pigments from different minerals are mixed with linseed oil or walnut oil. Oil paint is very durable, very luminous, and can be painted in layers. If you get really close to an old painting in a museum, you can even see these different layers. For a long time, it was thought that Jan van Eyck had invented oil paint. But long before van Eyck's time, this water-resistant paint had been used to coat ancient ships and medieval flags.

RENAISSANCE The Renaissance era lasted from about 1400 to the end of the 1500s. The origin of the word is French, and means "rebirth." During the Renaissance, people in Europe rediscovered the literature and art of antiquity. In addition, art and science blossomed during this time.

SILVERPOINT A silverpoint stylus was something like the pencil of the fifteenth century. It consists of a metal rod to which a silver tip is welded. The drawing is made by rubbing the silver off onto the paper. This technique creates very fine, light-gray lines similar to those made by an 8H pencil. Artists use silverpoint to draw on white-primed paper. The difficulty lies in the fact that you cannot simply rub out silverpoint mistakes as you can pencil errors. Either the mistakes remain visible, or you have to re-prime the paper. And so you have to be very confident and skilled when drawing in silverpoint.

INTAGLIO In this printing technique, an artist cuts a design into a metal printing plate. To make the print, the artist fills the plate with ink, wipes the raised areas of the plate clean, and then transfers the design onto paper. Etching is a kind of intaglio printing method. Woodcut, on the other hand, is a form of so-called relief printing. In this type of printing, the whole surface of the printing plate, except for the drawing, is carved away. Only the raised areas that form the design are then covered with ink and used to make the print. Linocut and potato printing, which you may have done at school, are also forms of relief printing.

POP ART This type of art developed in the 1950s and 1960s. Pop artists often took things that were "popular" or commonly used in their society—such as comic strips or soup cans—and depicted them in humorous ways in their artwork.

Answers to the quiz questions

Page 8:   It exists in the Palazzo Pubblico in Siena. This great picture was the work of Ambrogio Lorenzetti and was painted in around 1338.

Page 10:   It is the dome of Florence Cathedral. This dome was built between 1420 and 1436. With a diameter of over 40 meters (130 feet) and a height of 114 meters (374 feet), it is one of the biggest church domes in the world.

Page 22:   Dürer spent more than three months working on this engraving.

Page 33:   A Batman comic from 1939, in which Batman appears for the first time, was sold in 2010 for $1.1 million.

Library of Congress Control Number is available; British Library Cataloguing-in-Publication Data: a catalogue record for this book is available from the British Library; Deutsche Nationalbibliothek holds a record of this publication in the Deutsche Nationalbibliografie; detailed bibliographical data can be found under http://dnb.d-nb.de.

© Prestel Verlag, Munich • London • New York 2011
© for the works illustrated held by the artists or their legal heirs except for: Marcel Duchamp, Wassily Kandinsky, Franz Kline, Hans Naegeli, Jackson Pollock: © VG Bild-Kunst, Bonn 2011; Jacques Henri Lartigue: Jacques Henri Lartigue © Ministère de la Culture – France/AAJHL, Paris 2011; Hans Namuth: Courtesy Center for Creative Photography, University of Arizona © 1991 Hans Namuth Estate.

Photo credits:
akg: p. 9; bpk: cover top; Courtesy Center for Creative Photography, University of Arizona © 1991 Hans Namuth Estate: p. 40 bottom; Deutsches Museum für Karikatur und Zeichenkunst – Wilhelm Busch, Sammlung John Dirks: p. 33 top; Doris Kutschbach: p. 42 top, p. 44; Florian Heine: cover bottom, p. 12; Sisse Brimberg/National Geographic Stock: p. 5; Scala: p. 37.

Cover: Details from Details from Francesco di Giorgio Martini, Architectural Veduta, c. 1490/1500, Gemäldegalerie, Berlin; Édouard Manet (p. 30); Florian Heine, photograph.
Frontispiece: Detail from Andrea Mantegna, Camera degli Sposi, 1473, Mantua, Palazzo Ducale.

Prestel books are available worldwide. Please contact your nearest bookseller or one of the above addresses for information concerning your local distributor.

Prestel Publishing
A member of the Verlagsgruppe Random House GmbH
www.prestel.com

Translation: Jane Michael
Editor: Brad Finger

Project management: Doris Kutschbach
Picture editor: Katharina Knüppel
Production: Ulrike Wilke
Design: Michael Schmölzl,
agenten.und.freunde, Munich
Lithography: ReproLine Mediateam, Munich
Printing and Binding: Printer Trento, Trento

Verlagsgruppe Random House FSC®-DEU-0100
The FSC®-certified paper Eurobulk has been supplied by Papier Union.

ISBN 978-3-7913-7060-6